MY FIRST ENCYCLOPEDIA

An eye-catching series of information books designed to encourage young children to find out more about the world around them. Each one is carefully prepared by a subject specialist with the help of experienced writers and educational advisers.

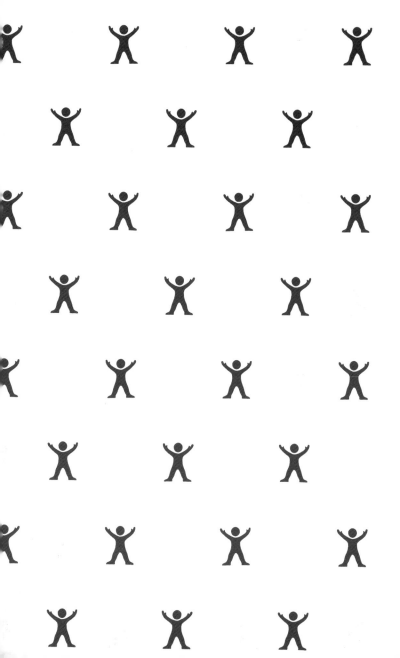

KINGFISHER
Kingfisher Publications Plc
New Penderel House, 283-288 High Holborn, London WC1V 7HZ

First published in paperback by Kingfisher Publications Plc 1994
2 4 6 8 10 9 7 5 3 1

1BP/0500/SF/(FR)/135MA

ISBN 1 85697 261 5

Phototypeset by Waveney Typesetters, Norwich
Printed in China

My Body

Kingfisher

Authors
Florence and Pierre-Olivier Wessels

Medical adviser
Dr Jean-Baptiste Carlander

Translator
Patricia Crampton

Series consultant
Brian Williams

Editor
Véronique Herbold

Designers
Gérard Finel and Martine Pfeiffer

Illustrators
Denise Bazin
Danièle Schulthess
Michèle Trumel

About this book 🧍 🧍 🧍

Every minute of the day, our bodies are busy working – while we wash and dress and eat, while we play and sleep. Different parts of the body work together to let us see, move and grow. How does this happen? What do the parts we can't see look like?

This book shows you how the human body works. It is arranged in sections, so you can read about the parts of the body (such as the brain and bones), the systems (such as the heart), and the senses (such as eyesight and hearing). It describes how babies grow into children and children into adults, and how we can look after our bodies sensibly. The human body is amazing, and this book is full of amazing information about it.

CONTENTS

LIFE STORY

THE SENSES

THE SYSTEMS

KEEPING FIT

My body

☀ One person, one body

There are five billion human beings on Earth. We all have a body made to the same design.

Human bodies are alike, but at the same time everyone is different! No one else is the same as you. You are unique.

✗ Differences

Children and adults, girls and boys, tall people and short people – we are all human beings, but we are all different.

Lots of details make us different from one another. The colour of our hair and skin... the shape of our eyes, ears, lips, nose, and chin... the way we stand, walk and talk.

✗ Likenesses

People who belong to the same family often look similar. Brothers and sisters are alike, and children resemble their parents.

Twin brothers and twin sisters can look almost exactly alike. You have to get really close to them to find out who is who.

This family tree shows three generations of one family:

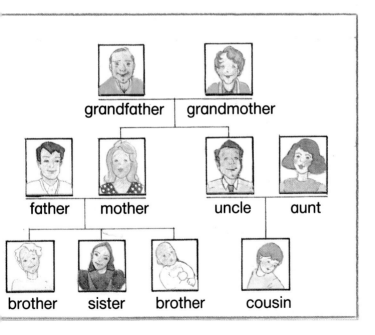

grandfather   grandmother

father   mother   uncle   aunt

brother   sister   brother   cousin

✗ A body for living

The body is like a clever machine that can do lots of things. It can laugh, cry, talk, walk, run and jump.

The body can also read, think, love, play, work and rest.

19

☓ A body for everywhere

People want to go every-
where, and they can.

People can travel high in the sky, explore space, and dive down through the ocean.

People live in rainforests and towns, in frozen lands and hot deserts. The human body has adapted or changed to live in different conditions.

✗ The history of the body

The story of the human body began three and a half million years ago.

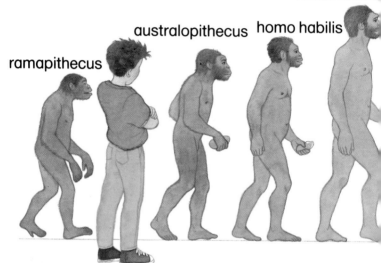

ramapithecus australopithecus homo habilis homo erectu

Since then, the human body has changed.

Scientists find bones of people who lived long ago, and study the differences between their bodies and ours.

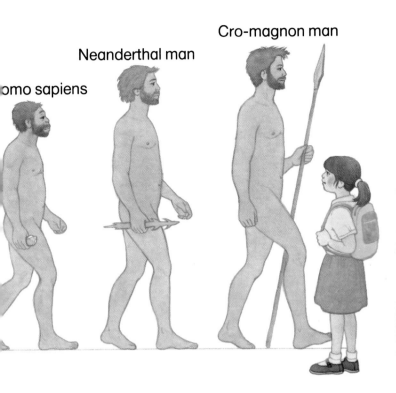

Cro-magnon man

Neanderthal man

omo sapiens

he change from the first humans to
urselves is called evolution.

Jowadays an eight-year-old child is as tall
s an adult australopithecus. She knows
nuch more than the first humans knew.
he lives three or four times longer. This is
ecause she lives in better conditions.

Amazing facts

Like cats and whales, human beings are mammals. All mammal mothers make milk in their bodies to feed their babies.

A double is someone who looks exactly like another person, without being his or her twin.

The science which studies the similarities between parents and their children is called genetics.

The first true human beings lived about two million years ago, in Africa. Scientists call this type homo habilis.

From head

to foot

 # Body parts

The human body has a head, a torso, two upper limbs which are our arms, and two lower limbs which are our legs.

These parts of the body help it to do different things.

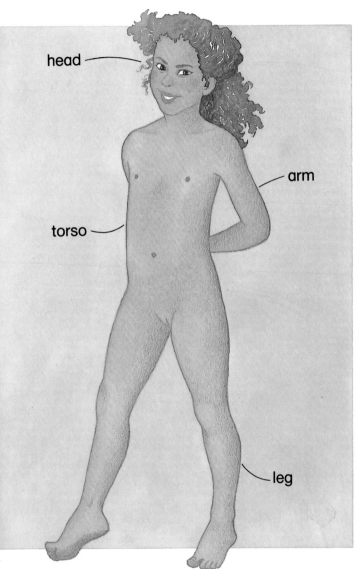

head

arm

torso

leg

 # The skin

Skin covers the whole body.

Skin keeps the parts
inside us safe.

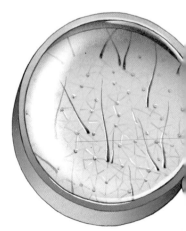

Skin is very sensitive
to the sun's rays
and may get
burned. Suncream
protects it.

Grazed skin bleeds.
The wound must be cleaned,
to get rid of dirt and germs.
A bandage keeps the wound clean and dry.
The blood dries and forms a scab. New skin
grows under the scab, and the scab falls off.

✊ Marks on the skin

Skin has pigments or colouring called melanin. Melanin helps protect the ski from sunlight. Freckles often appear on fair ski that has been in the sun They are patches of extra melanin.

Moles are permanent patches of melanin.

Sometimes our faces change colour! People turr red with embarrassment, and white with shock.

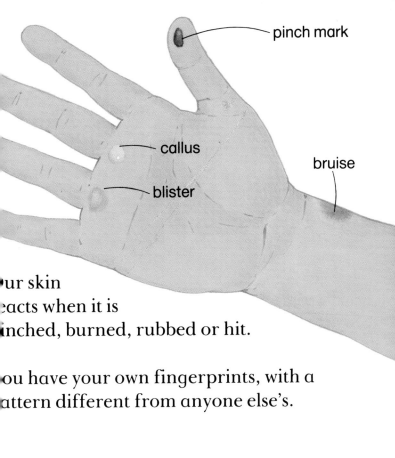

- pinch mark
- callus
- bruise
- blister

ur skin
eacts when it is
inched, burned, rubbed or hit.

ou have your own fingerprints, with a
attern different from anyone else's.

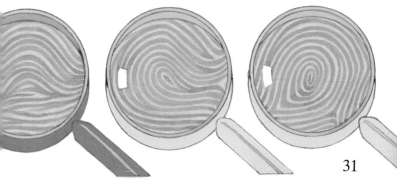

31

✋Hair and nails

We have hair all over our bodies, except for our palms and the soles of our feet.

You see only part of the hair. The rest is under the skin. It is called the root. When you are cold, a little muscle pulls the hair upright. You have goose pimples!

normal hair

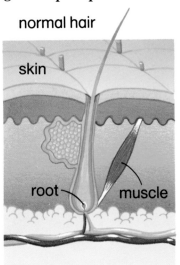

skin

root — muscle

hair standing | on end

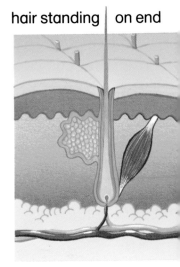

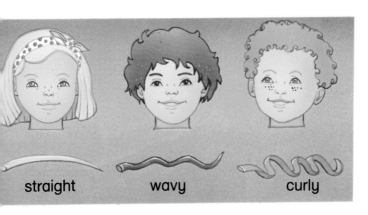

straight   wavy   curly

air grows out of tiny holes in our skin.
)me people's hair grows straight, some
avy and some curly.

air is made of keratin. So are our nails.
ails protect our toes and fingertips.

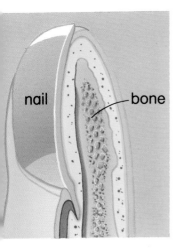

nail   bone

A cat's claws
are its nails.

 # Muscles

Under our skin are the muscles. We use muscles whenever we move.

Muscles are joined to bones. They contract, or tighten, to pull a bone, and relax, or loosen, to release it.

We have more than 650 muscles in our bodies. They move every part of the body, not just bones. The muscles in our face help us to smile, frown, wink and chew. The muscles in our chest help us to breathe.

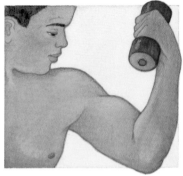

Muscles grow bigger and stronger with exercise and training.

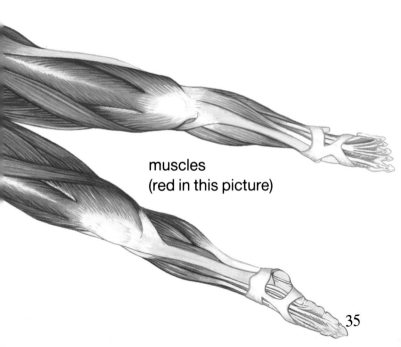

muscles
(red in this picture)

The skeleton

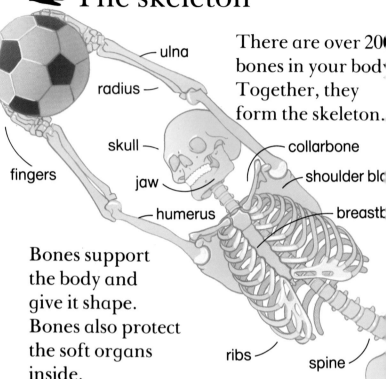

ulna

radius

skull

jaw

fingers

humerus

collarbone

shoulder bl

breastb

ribs

spine

There are over 20(
bones in your bod'
Together, they
form the skeleton.

Bones support
the body and
give it shape.
Bones also protect
the soft organs
inside.

Your nose feels har
but it is not all bone.
The tip of it is a
delicate piece of
cartilage or gristle.

As you grow up,
your bones grow
longer and
thicker. So you
grow taller and
heavier too.

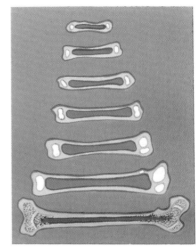

hip

thigh

kneecap

toes

tibia

heel

fibula

37

☚ Bones and joints

Some bones fit together, others slide over each other. Our knees, spine, shoulders and elbows are some of the joints where bones meet.

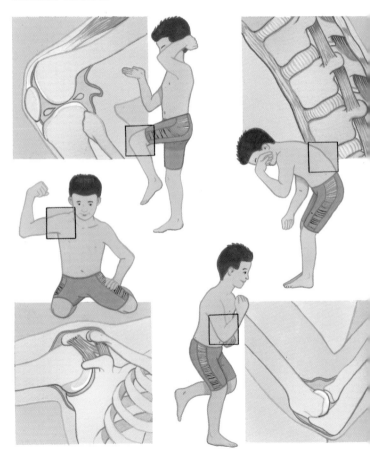

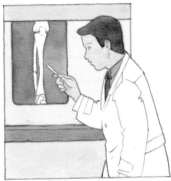

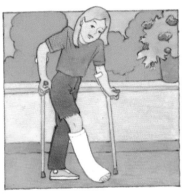

lthough bones are strong, they may break
a fall. The doctor looks at the fracture,
break, on an X-ray photograph.

hen the injured part of the body may be
rapped in plaster, to hold the bone
raight while it grows back together again.

✋ The brain

The brain inside your head is the most important part of your body.

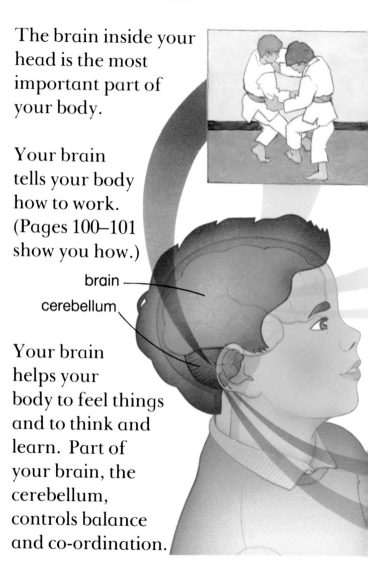

Your brain tells your body how to work. (Pages 100–101 show you how.)

brain —

cerebellum

Your brain helps your body to feel things and to think and learn. Part of your brain, the cerebellum, controls balance and co-ordination.

41

← Other organs

The brain is one of the soft organs inside your body. The other organs all have special tasks of their own. They help the body to work properly.

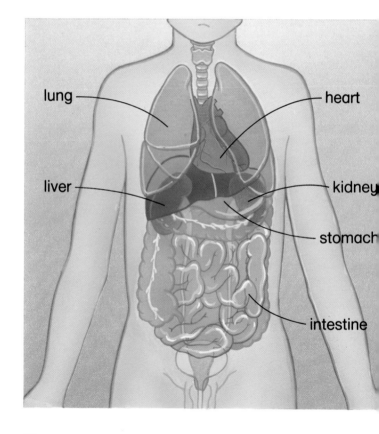

lung

heart

liver

kidney

stomach

intestine

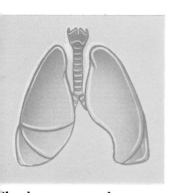

The lungs supply blood with oxygen.

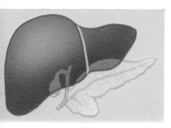

The liver helps us to digest our food.

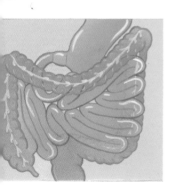

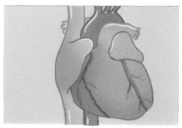

The heart pumps blood around the body.

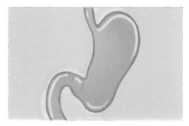

The stomach mashes food into a pulp.

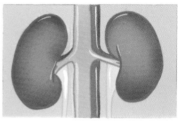

◀ The intestines pass food into the blood.

▲ Two kidneys help to get rid of waste.

Amazing facts

 More than 200 muscles go into action when you take a step, but only 15 when you smile!

We have 300 bones at birth, but only 208 when we are adults. This is because some bones join together as we grow up.

Fingernails grow twice as fast as toenails, about one millimetre a week. Human nails and hair are made of keratin. So are reptiles' scales and birds' feathers.

We lose about fifty hairs every day.

Life story

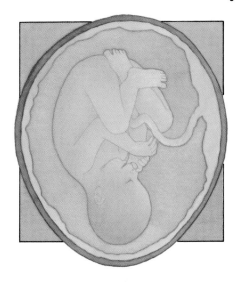

🐾 Where do you come fr⟨

The body is made of millions of tiny living parts called cells – bone cells and skin cells, brain cells and blood cells, cells for every part of your body.

But we all began as just one cell inside our mother's body, before we were born. Every baby is made by a man and a woman. They are the baby's parents.

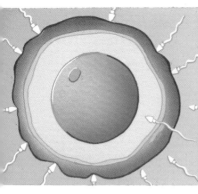

A sperm from the
father enters an egg
inside the mother.

Now the egg is
fertilized. It is
the first cell
of the baby.

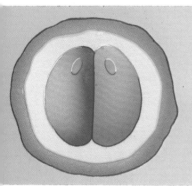

The egg is even
smaller than a dot
made by a pencil.

The egg splits into
two cells, and then
into four, and so on.

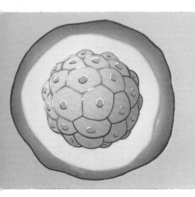

So the egg grows
bigger and bigger.

The egg moves to a
part of the mother
called the womb.
This is the start of
her pregnancy.

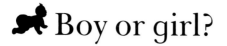 Boy or girl?

What will the baby look like? The answer is in the genes.

Genes are special instructions in each cell which tell it what to do. Everyone has two sets of genes, one from the father's sperm and one from the mother's egg. The colour of the baby's hair and eyes, how tall it will grow, whether it is a boy or a girl – everything is decided by the genes.

A doctor or a midwife checks that the pregnancy is going well. A scanning machine shows the baby inside the womb. If they want to, the parents can find out if the baby is a boy or a girl.

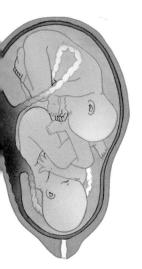

Sometimes a mother has two babies from one egg. These are identical twins, two boys or two girls who will look just like each other.

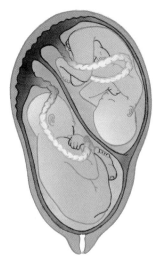

Or she may have twins from two eggs. These twins are not identical.

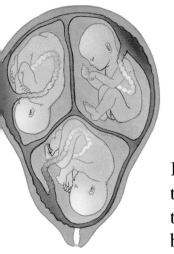

It is very rare, but there may even be three, four, five or six babies!

🐾 Nine months for a bab

The baby grows in a bag of war
liquid in the mother's womb. It gets d
the food and oxygen it needs from i
mother's body, through a tube calle
the umbilical cor

At one month, the baby's heart
beating. The baby is no bigg
than a pe

At three months, it is about s
centimetres long and lool
more like a bab

At four months, it cc
move abou

At five months,
it sucks its thumb.

At six months, it can
hear sounds.

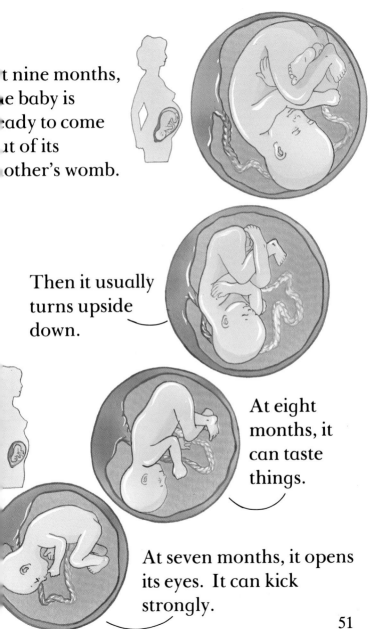

t nine months,
e baby is
ady to come
ut of its
other's womb.

Then it usually
turns upside
down.

At eight
months, it
can taste
things.

At seven months, it opens
its eyes. It can kick
strongly.

51

The birth

When the baby is ready to be born, the mother can go to hospital to give birth.
Her muscles help to push the baby out. Usually the baby comes out head first.

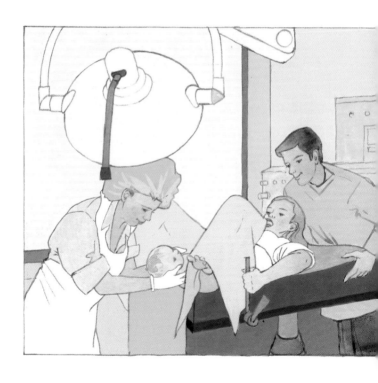

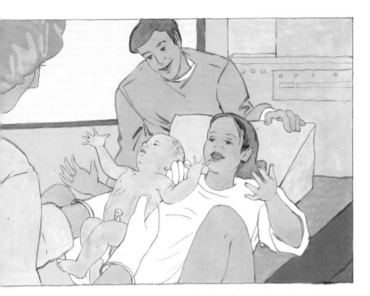

he doctor or the midwife helps the baby to
ome out. The baby takes its first breath
nd cries. It does not need the umbilical
ord after it is born. So the cord is cut off.

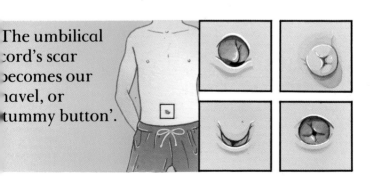

The umbilical
cord's scar
becomes our
navel, or
'tummy button'.

🐱 Baby days

A brand-new baby needs a lot of care and love.

At first, it sleeps a lot. When it is hungry, it cries for its mother's milk or its bottle.

The baby likes being held by its parents.
It recognizes their voices and their smell.

The baby looks
at things
nearby. It
enjoys its bath
and clean
nappies, and
smiles.

Vaccinations
protect the baby
from diseases.

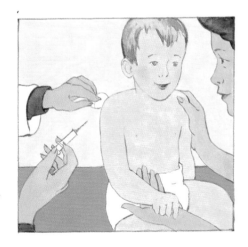

Childhood

The baby grows. It do
more and more things
by itself.

it walks,

It sits up,

it eats.

The baby grows into a child. Children are learning things all the time: riding their first bike, going to school, playing games and meeting other people.

🐾 Growing up

Children grow into teenagers and adults. By the time they are about eighteen years old, their bodies have stopped growing.

eople start work, and they fall in love.

they want to, a man and woman can live gether and start a family.

Growing old

People have busy lives, working, studying and bringing up a family.

As the body grows older, the muscles get weaker, so they get tired more easily.

When people die, those who loved them can remember them long after they have gone.

Amazing facts

An adult body has about 50 billion cells – remember, all those cells begin with just one cell, the fertilized egg.

The egg is the biggest cell in the bod But it is only one fifth of a millimetre wide.

Which lives longest: a dog, a human or an elephant? A human! The oldest person ever lived to be 121.

Around the world, 140 babies are born every minute.

The senses

👁 Hearing

We hear sounds all the time. They are invisible waves in the air. Some sounds are pleasant, some are not. But they all give us information about the world around us.

e can see only
rt of the ear.
he rest is inside
e head. Sounds
ter the ear, and
ake the
rdrum vibrate.
his makes tiny
nes move.
hen a nerve
rries the
essage to
e brain.

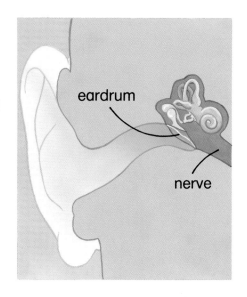

The brain tells us what we
are hearing.

A hearing aid makes sounds
louder, to help people who
cannot hear well.

👁 Smell

We use the nose for breathing, and for smelling. Smells float in the air. Although they are invisible, we can tell what they are. We like some smells, but not others!

hen a smell
aches the back
your nose,
rves carry the
formation to the
ain. The brain
cides what the
ell is.

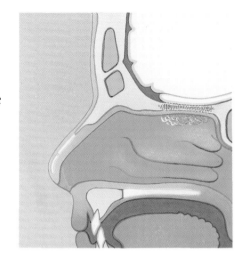

Some doctors look
after only the
ears, nose and
throat.

Our sense of smell
elps our sense of
aste. That is why it
difficult to taste
hings when you
ave a cold and
blocked-up
ose.

👁 Touch

When we touch things, we can feel them.
Our skin feels the heat of a cup of cocoa,
the cold of ice, the prick of a thorn, the
softness of a cat's fur.

Tiny nerves in the skin send messages about things we touch to the brain.

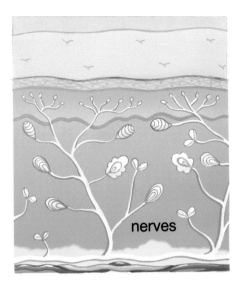

nerves

reading in braille

A blind person can read and write braille, by using her sense of touch.

writing in braille

The pianist controls the pressure of his fingers on the keys to play loudly or softly.

👁 Taste

The tongue feels heat and cold, pain and different tastes.

sweet   salty

There are thousands of little bumps called taste buds all over your tongue. Inside the buds are nerves that send messages to the brain about what you are eating.

There are four types of taste: sweet, salty, bitter and sour. The tongue has areas which are especially good at recognizing each one of these tastes.

he best way to taste ice cream is to lick it
ith the tip of your tongue, which is the best
art for picking up sweet tastes.

our

bitter

he back of the tongue recognizes bitter
astes.

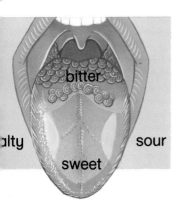

The sides
recognize sour
and salty tastes.

The front
recognizes sweet
tastes.

71

👁 Sight

We see the world around us with our eyes. They help us to recognize shape, height, distance and colour.

very time you blink, your eyelids spread ears over your eyes, to keep them moist nd clean.

he eye is shaped like a ball. It has muscles tached to it, so it can move up and down and le to side.

ght bounces off e things you ok at and enters ur eye through e pupil. Nerves the retina send essages to the ain. The brain lls you what u see.

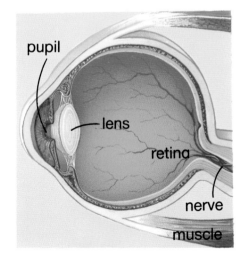

pupil

lens

retina

nerve

muscle

👁 The eyes

When it is dark your pupils grow larger, to let in more light. This helps you see better.

In the mountains, you need dark glasses to protect your eyes against the glare of sunlight on the snow.

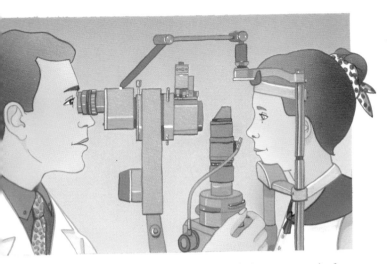

he optician examines eyes with a special
strument. He sees through the pupil to
e retina at the back of the eye.

Not everyone
can see well.
Some people
wear glasses or
contact lenses to
improve their
eyesight.

Blind people find
their way with a
white stick.

👁 The voice

We can talk, shout, laugh and sing. The sounds are made by vocal cords in our throats. We form words by moving our tongue, lips and jaws.

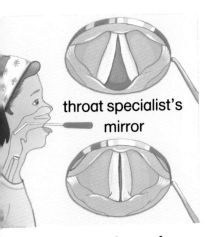

throat specialist's mirror

Our vocal cords are two stretchy flaps. The air we breathe out makes them vibrate. This is what produces sounds.

The harder we breathe out, the louder our voice is. If you put your fingers on your throat while you sing, you can feel the vibrations.

Some people cannot speak. They use sign language instead.

👁 Body talk

The body has a silent language of its own.
It can express our feelings without words.

he way people stand, the gestures they
ake with their hands, and the expressions
ι their faces all send clear messages.
'hen we are happy, we look different from
hen we are sad.

👁 When you are ill

When we are ill, we may have a high temperature, a cough, spots, or aches and pains. These are signs that the body is being attacked by germs.

When the body is fighting off invading germs, it works harder and the heart beats faster. The body's temperature rises.

he doctor examines you to find out which
art of you the germs are attacking.
he listens to your heart and lungs with a
ethoscope, looks in your ears and throat,
1d asks you questions. Then the doctor
ecides if you need anything to help you
t better.

You may need
medicine to fight
against the germs.

👁 Out of danger

Diseases such as chickenpox are very catching. But you catch some of them only once. After that, the body recognizes the disease and protects itself against it.

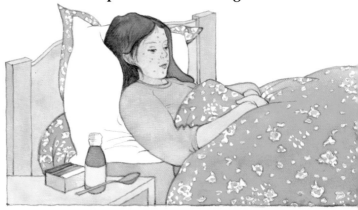

So you can visit a friend who has chickenpox if you have already had it.

he brain stores information. This is called
emory. It is what helps you to talk, learn
d think.

The brain helps
us to avoid
accidents. We
remember to take
care when we
cross the road.

Amazing facts

Your ears help you to keep your balance. When you move, liquid in your ear moves and sets off nerves that tell your brain about the position of your body.

Fingertips are very sensitive. The skin there has more nerve endings than the skin on other parts of the body.

Some people are colour-blind. This means they confuse colours. For example, they may think green is red and red is green.

People mostly rely on sight to find things. Dogs use their noses more. Bats hunt at night, so they need to hear well.

A voice can be so high-pitched that sound cracks a crystal glass!

The systems

Eating for energy

We eat food because it gives our bodies energy. People eat many kinds of food, but our bodies digest everything in the same way.

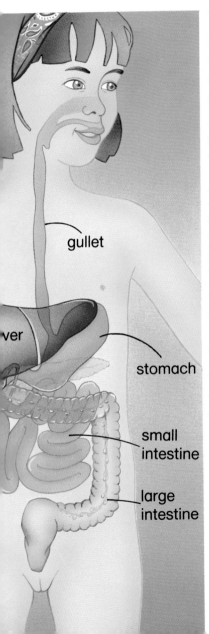

gullet

ver

stomach

small
intestine

large
intestine

When you swallow food, it moves down a tube into the stomach. The stomach mashes it into pulp. Next, it is squeezed along your intestines.

Now the food is digested, and it passes through the intestine into the blood. The blood takes it around your body.

The body gets rid of the food it cannot use when we go to the lavatory.

 # Teeth

We bite into food and chew it with our teeth so it is easier to swallow and digest. The sharp incisors at the front are for cutting. Pointed canines at the sides are for tearing. Big molars at the back are for crushing.

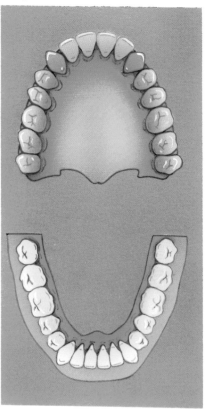

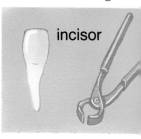

incisor

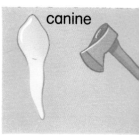

canine

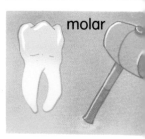

molar

hard layer of
enamel covers
the dentine.
Inside this is the
pulp, the
sensitive part.
Under the gum,
each tooth has a
root that holds
it in place in the
jaw bone.

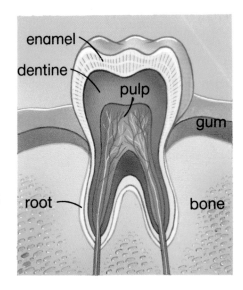

When we are
about six
years old, our
first teeth
become loose
and fall out.

They make
room for the
larger teeth
that are
growing
underneath.

89

At the dentist's

The dentist looks after our teeth. If he fin
a decaying tooth with a hole, he removes
the decay and fills the hole with hard past

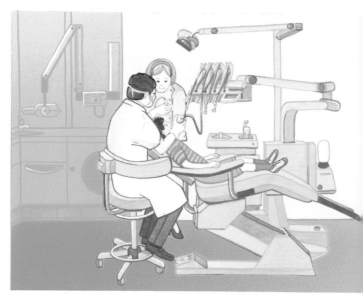

Crooked teeth can be straightened by wearing
brace or plate.

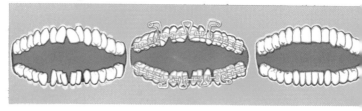

rushing your teeth
r three minutes
ice a day helps to
event decay.

hen you brush
ur teeth, you get
d of the food
raps and germs
at cause decay.

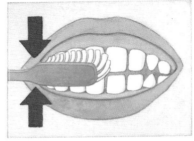

ways brush from
nk to white, from
e gums to the
eth.

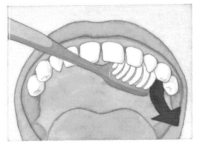

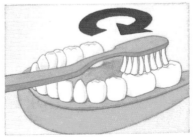

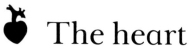 # The heart

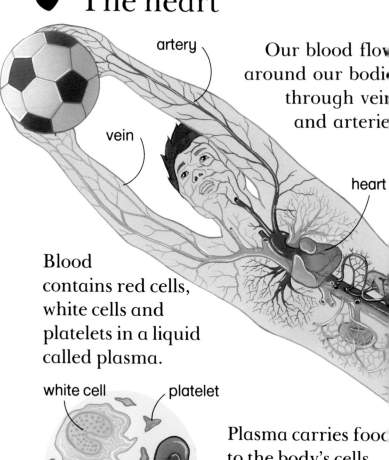

artery

vein

heart

Our blood flow
around our bodie
through vein
and arterie

Blood
contains red cells,
white cells and
platelets in a liquid
called plasma.

white cell   platelet

plasma   red cell

Plasma carries foo
to the body's cells.
Red cells carry
oxygen. White cells
kill germs. Platelets
help to stop bleedin

he heart is a
ollow muscle. As it
ontracts or beats,
pumps blood
round the body.

our heart works
l day and all
ght, without
opping.

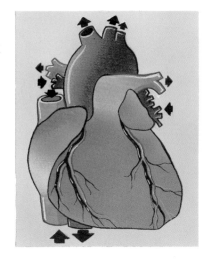

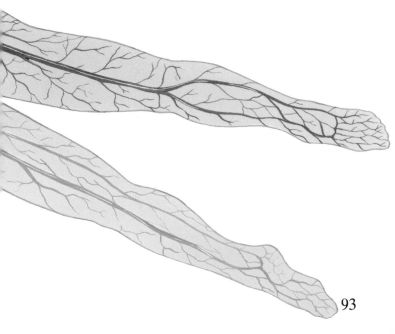

Breathing

We need oxygen to stay alive. Our lungs take oxygen from the air we breathe. Our blood takes the oxygen from the lungs and carries it to the rest of the body.

It is impossible to stay under water without a snorkel or air tanks, because there is no air to breathe.

When you breathe in through your nose or your mouth, air goes down your windpipe and into your lungs.

Blood travels through your lungs and collects oxygen from them. Blood also carries used air back to the lungs.

When you breathe out, your lungs push the used air back out through your nose or your mouth.

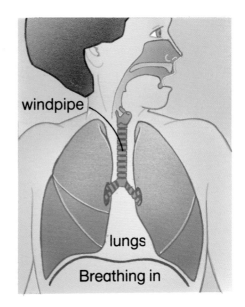

windpipe

lungs

Breathing in

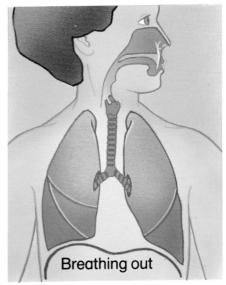

Breathing out

Male and female

Men and women have different organs for making a baby.

A woman has:
● two ovaries that produce an egg each month;
● two tubes that link the ovaries to the womb;
● the womb, where the fertilized egg grows into a baby;
● the vagina.

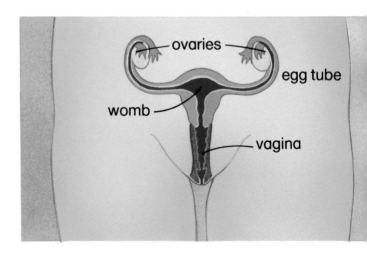

ovaries

egg tube

womb

vagina

man has:
two testicles that make sperm;
two tubes that pass sperm to the penis;
the penis.

1ese organs are ready to make a baby
ly after adolescence, when we grow into
en and women.

ou can find out how a baby is made if you
rn back to page 46.

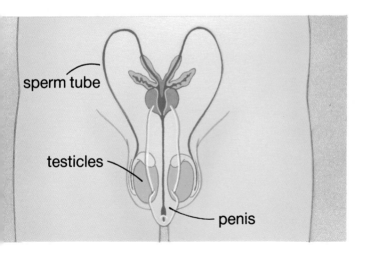

Getting rid of waste

As your body works, it creates waste products. The body gets rid of them in several ways. We breathe out used air. Our sweat gets rid of salt and other waste.

ur kidneys
so get rid of
aste.

ood flows
rough the
dneys. They
parate water,
t and other
aste from the
ood. This waste
urned into
ine and stored
a pouch called
e bladder.

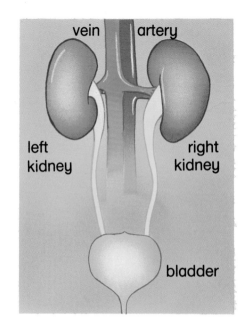

When the bladder is full, we have to go to
e lavatory.

The nervous system

A network of nerves links every part of the body with the brain.

From our senses, the nerves receive information about our bodies and the world around us.

The nerves send the information as electric signals to the spinal cord. This is a thick bundle of nerves down the middle of our backs. The spinal cord carries the signals up to the brain.

The brain sorts out the information. It sends commands along other nerves to tell the body's organs and muscles how to react.

All of this happens very quickly, in less than a second.

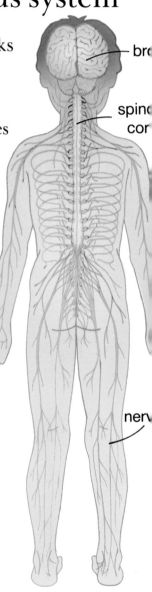

br

spin
cor

ner

ur nervous system helps us to use
ır senses, to think, remember and
ɑn, and to move.

ɔmetimes we do things without thinking.
hen you touch something sharp, your hand
ll jerk away, without waiting for a message
om the brain. This is called reflex action.

Amazing facts

 As we grow up, we have more blood. A new-born baby has less than half a litre of blood, an eight year old has about 1.75 litres and adults have between 5 and 6 litre

It takes about one minute for blood to flow from the heart to your toes and ba again. To pump blood around your body, your heart beats about 70 times per minut An elephant's heart beats only 25 times pe minute. A mouse's heart beats 500 times per minute.

You take about 23,000 breaths each do

When you sneeze, air rushes out of your nose at about 160 kilometres per hou

The fastest nerve signals travel at 400 kilometres per hour. That is about the same speed as a racing car.

Keeping

fit

☺ Sleep

While you are asleep, your body keeps working, like a town at night.

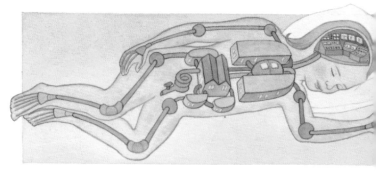

But it works more slowly, so that it can rest and grow.

ost children sleep for about twelve hours
very night. Babies need more sleep, and
dults need less.

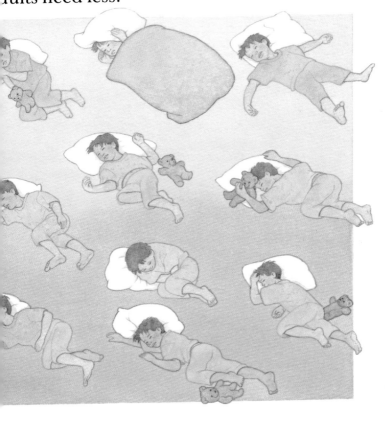

ou do not lie completely still all night.
ou change position many times.

☺ Dreams and nightmar

While we are asleep we have dreams. The
stories in our dreams seem real while we a
asleep. But we don't always remember
them when we wake up.

Nightmares are frightening dreams.
Some nightmares are so frightening that
they wake us up.
But nightmares are useful because they use
up some of the unhappiness and worries
we have in real life.

☺ Playing games

We make full use of our bodies when we play games. Physical exercise helps us to grow stronger. With regular exercise, our bodies become fitter and less easily tired.

...orts are fun. Whichever sport we choose,
...e have to follow the rules and concentrate
... do well. On our own or in a team, we
...ould play so that everybody has fun.

☺ Healthy meals

Your food should give your body what it needs to keep working. There are three main groups of food. You can help your body by eating food from each group, and by drinking enough water.

These are the three groups. Each type of food acts on the body in a particular way.

Proteins build and repair cells so that the body can grow and stay strong.

Carbohydrates supply energy to keep the body going.

Fats store energy for the body to use, but we shouldn't eat too much fat.

☺ Vitamins

The body needs vitamins to work smoothly.
These six vitamins are in our food.

VITAMIN A
for good
eyesight and
healthy skin.

VITAMIN B
to help turn food
into energy, and fo
healthy skin and n

VITAMIN C
to help us recover
from illness quickly,
and to help wounds
heal.

is important to eat vitamins every day,
cause our bodies do not produce
ough of them all.

TAMIN D
help us grow.

VITAMIN E
to help the body's
cells stay strong.

TAMIN K
help our blood
t, so that we
n't bleed too
ch if we get a cut.

☺ Keeping clean

Our skin gets dirty. It is important to wash every day, because soap and water help to get rid of any germs. It is also nice for other people if we are clean and smell fresh.

For the same reason, we change out of our clothes and wash them, and we put on clean clothes.

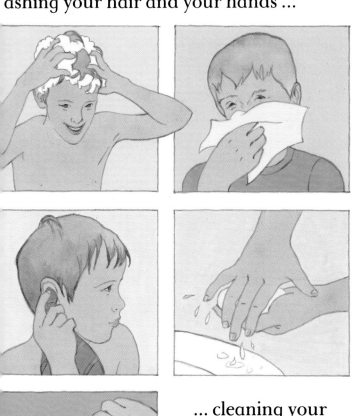

... cleaning your ears, cutting your nails, blowing your nose and brushing your teeth are all part of keeping clean.

☺ Dressing up

Clothes help the body to stay at the right temperature. We wear more clothes in cold weather than we do in hot weather. Clothes also protect our bodies. For example, we wear a helmet and pads when we play some sports.

ople dress up to make themselves look
ce and feel good. We can choose a new
irstyle, wear some jewellery and put on
me make-up, or wear a tie.

There are lots of
styles and fashions
to choose from.
People dress up the
way they like best.

☺ A happy life

Love and friendship and respect for each other make life happy for everyone.

We express these feelings with our bodies –
with a cuddle, a kiss, a hug, a smile, or an
outstretched hand.

Funny phrases

☺ If you want to describe a moment of great excitement or fear, you can say: "*My heart was in my mouth!*" Parts of the body are often used in phrases like this. Here ar some more examples:

☺ When you try to remember the right word, it's often *on the tip of your tongue.*

☺ *To put your foot in it* means to make a blunder. But if things go wrong, just *keep your hair on* or stay cool!

☺ *The apple of your eye* is your favourite person.

☺ When something costs *an arm and a leg*, it is very expensive.

NDEX

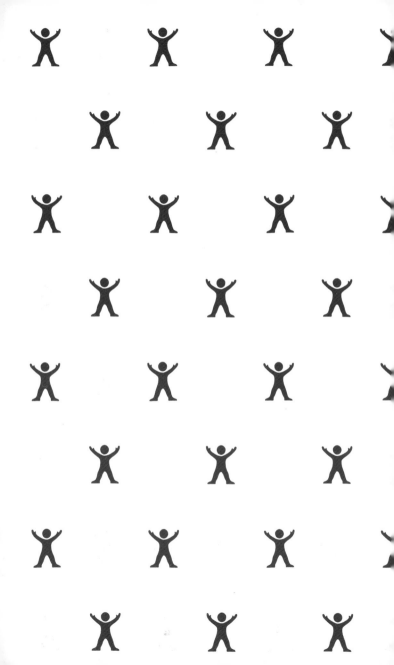

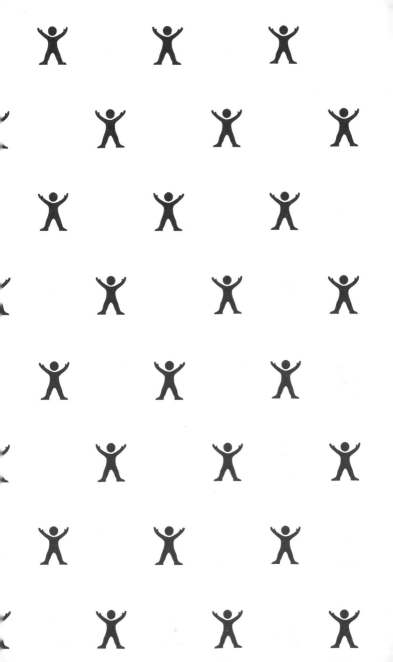